IT'S TIME TO LEARN ABOUT BUTTERFLY FISH

It's Time to Learn about Butterfly Fish

Walter the Educator

Silent King Books
A WhichHead Entertainment Imprint

Copyright © 2025 by Walter the Educator

All rights reserved. No part of this book may be reproduced in any manner whatsoever without written per- mission except in the case of brief quotations embodied in critical articles and reviews.

First Printing, 2024

Disclaimer

This book is a literary work; the story is not about specific persons, locations, situations, and/or circumstances unless mentioned in a historical context. Any resemblance to real persons, locations, situations, and/or circumstances is coincidental. This book is for entertainment and informational purposes only. The author and publisher offer this information without warranties expressed or implied. No matter the grounds, neither the author nor the publisher will be accountable for any losses, injuries, or other damages caused by the reader's use of this book. The use of this book acknowledges an understanding and acceptance of this disclaimer.

It's Time to Learn about Butterfly Fish is a collectible early learning book by Walter the Educator suitable for all ages belonging to Walter the Educator's Time to Eat Book Series. Collect more books at WaltertheEducator.com

USE THE EXTRA SPACE TO TAKE NOTES AND DOCUMENT YOUR MEMORIES

BUTTERFLY FISH

In the ocean, bright and blue,

It's Time to Learn about
Butterfly Fish

Lives a fish with colors true.

The Butterfly Fish, small and bright,

With fins that shimmer in the light.

It's not a bug, though named the same,

Butterfly Fish is its name!

With patterns like a butterfly's wings,

It swims and sways and does cool things.

It loves warm waters near coral reefs,

Where waves are calm and life's a feast.

Hiding in rocks and coral caves,

It swims through tunnels, twists, and waves.

Its body's thin, like a pancake wide,

So it can sneak and smoothly glide.

With stripes and spots from head to tail,

It blends right in, a perfect veil!

It's Time to Learn about Butterfly Fish

Butterfly Fish love tasty treats,

Tiny worms and shrimp they eat.

They use their snout, so long and thin,

To poke for food tucked deep within.

Some have a spot near their tail,

A clever trick that never fails!

Predators think that's the head,

While the fish swims safely ahead.

Butterfly Fish live in pairs,

Swimming with a friend who cares.

They stick together every day,

Dancing through the ocean spray.

Their fins can flap like wings in flight,

Gliding gently, what a sight!

With colors yellow, white, and black,

It's Time to Learn about Butterfly Fish

They shine like treasure in a pack.

They help keep coral reefs so clean,

Eating algae in between.

A helpful fish, both small and bright,

Keeping reefs healthy, day and night.

So next time you explore the sea,

Look for Butterfly Fish with glee.

A fish so pretty, quick, and small,

It's Time to Learn about Butterfly Fish

The Butterfly Fish, loved by all!

ABOUT THE CREATOR

Walter the Educator is one of the pseudonyms for Walter Anderson. Formally educated in Chemistry, Business, and Education, he is an educator, an author, a diverse entrepreneur, and he is the son of a disabled war veteran. "Walter the Educator" shares his time between educating and creating. He holds interests and owns several creative projects that entertain, enlighten, enhance, and educate, hoping to inspire and motivate you. Follow, find new works, and stay up to date with Walter the Educator™

at WaltertheEducator.com

www.ingramcontent.com/pod-product-compliance
Lightning Source LLC
LaVergne TN
LVHW051919060526
838201LV00060B/4080